EASA Private Pilot Licence & Light Aircraft Pilot Licence
Aeroplane & Helicopter
Air Law Revision Guide

ISBN 9781906 559540

Airplan Flight Equipment

This book is intended to be a study aid to the Air Law Theoretical Knowledge element of the EASA PPL & LAPL (A & H) course. It does not in any way replace or overrule the instruction you will receive from a flight instructor at an approved or registered training organisation.

Nothing in this publication overrules or supersedes EASA regulations or EU rules and other documents published by a competent authority; the flight manual/pilot's operating handbook for the aircraft being flown; the pilot order book or operations manual; training syllabus; or the general provisions of good airmanship and safe flying practice.

First Edition 2013
Revised edition 2015

EASA Private Pilot Licence & Light Aircraft Pilot Licence
Aeroplane & Helicopter
Air Law Revision Guide

ISBN 9781906 559540

Airplan Flight Equipment
1a Ringway Trading Estate
Shadowmoss Road
Manchester M22 5LH
Tel: 0161 499 0023
Fax: 0161 499 0298
www.afeonline.com

CONTENTS

Intentionally Left Blank

International Law

According to ICAO's 'Chicago' convention:
- Every state has complete and exclusive **sovereignty** over airspace above its territory.

  - The **territory** of a state is the land areas and adjacent territorial waters under the sovereignty, protection or mandate of the state.

  - A state may require arriving, crossing and departing aircraft to route via a **designated customs airport**.

  - Every aircraft flying over a state's territory, and every aircraft carrying a territory's nationality mark - wherever it is - must comply with that territory's **rules of the air**.

  - Every aircraft engaged in international navigation must have a valid **Certificate of Airworthiness** issued by the state in which it is registered.

  - The pilot and crew of every aircraft engaged in international navigation must have **certificates of competency and licences** issued or validated by the state in which the aircraft is registered.

  - No aircraft or personnel with **endorsed licences or certificates** will engage in international navigation except with the permission of the state or states whose territory is entered. An endorsed licence or certificate will state why the aircraft or pilot does not meet international standards.

Airworthiness of Aircraft (Annex 8)

A **Certificate of Airworthiness** may be invalidated if an aircraft is repaired or modified in some way which is not approved, if the aircraft is operated outside the operating limits prescribed in the Pilot's Operating Handbook / Flight Manual (POH/FM), or if the aircraft is not maintained in accordance with an approved maintenance schedule.
An aircraft's C of A is normally required to be carried on board an aircraft making an international flight.

Aircraft Nationality and Registration (Annex 7)

The state of registry is the state on whose register an aircraft is entered.

According to ICAO recommendations the **Certificate of Registration** should be carried in the aircraft at all times.

Personnel Licencing (Annex 1)

The basic privilege of the holder of a Private Pilot Licence (PPL) is to act without remuneration as Pilot In Command (PIC) or co-pilot on aeroplanes, helicopters or Touring Motor Gliders (as appropriate) engaged in non-commercial operations.

An EASA PPL holder is required to hold at least a PART-Med Class 1 or Class 2 **medical certificate**.

An EASA LAPL holder is required to hold at least a LAPL medical certificate.

A medical certificate holder must seek advice upon becoming aware of:

- a hospital or clinic admission for more than 12 hours;
- a surgical operation or invasive procedure;
- the regular use of medication; or
- the need to regularly use correcting lenses.

and must inform the competent authority in writing of any significant personal injury involving incapacity to function as a member of a flight crew, or of becoming pregnant. In the case of an illness throughout a period of 21 days or more, the authority must be informed in writing as soon as the period of 21 days has elapsed. The medical certificate will then be considered as suspended.

Flight time to be credited for a licence or rating must be flown in the same category of aircraft for which the licence or rating is sought.

To act as Pilot In Command (PIC) whilst **carrying passengers**, a PPL or LAPL holder must have made three take-offs and three landings as the sole manipulator of the controls, in an aircraft of the same type or class, within the preceding 90 days.

In the UK, for the purposes of pilot licencing **night** is defined as the period from half an hour after sunset until half an hour before sunrise. The ICAO and EASA definition of night is the hours between the end of evening civil twilight and the beginning of morning civil twilight.

Single-pilot, single-engine aeroplane class ratings are valid for two years. To retain validity the holder must:

- pass a proficiency check within the three months immediately preceding the expiry of the rating;

OR

- within 12 months preceding rating expiry complete 12 hours of flight time, including six hours PIC time and 12 take-offs and landings and also complete a training flight of at least one hour with a flight instructor within the 12 months preceding the expiry of the rating. This training flight may be replaced by any other proficiency check or skill test for a class or type rating.

Rules of the Air (annex 2)

Where aircraft are converging in the air, the aircraft on the right has right of way: *"On the right, in the right"*. An aircraft which has right of way should maintain heading and speed.

Order of precedence in the air:

1.	Balloons
2.	Gliders (sailplanes)
3.	Airships
4.	power-driven, heavier than air aircraft (aeroplanes, helicopters etc.)
Powered aircraft give way to aircraft towing gliders or objects	

Converging aircraft: The aircraft on the right has right of way, **"On the right, in the right".** The aircraft giving way must avoid passing over, under or in front of the other aircraft, unless it passes well clear

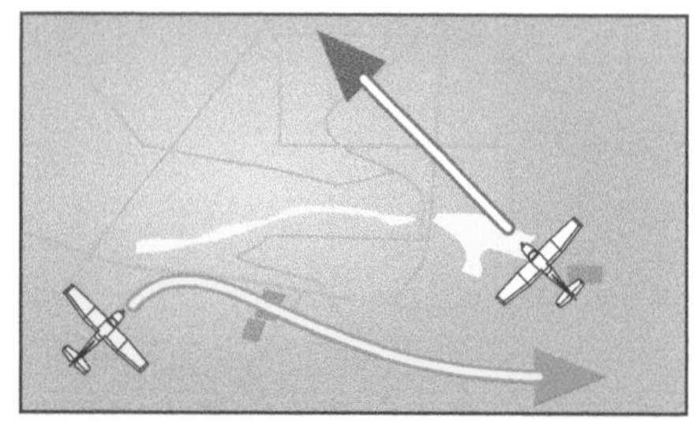

Head On: Both aircraft turn to the right

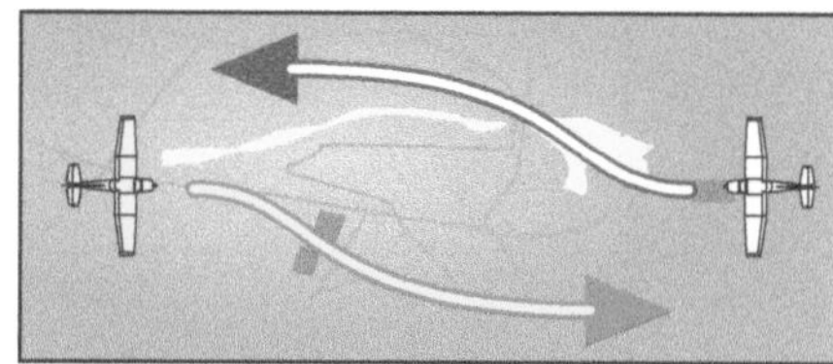

Overtaking: The overtaking aircraft turns to the right. Overtaking exists while the overtaking aircraft is within 70° of the centreline of the overtaken aircraft

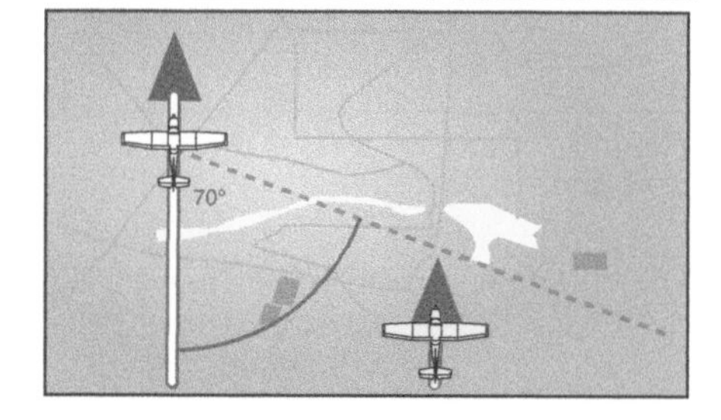

Where landings and take-offs are **not** confined to a runway, an aircraft taking-off must leave on its left an aircraft which has taken off or is about to take-off and an aircraft landing must leave on its left an aircraft which has landed.

Rule of Precedence on the ground:

1.	Aircraft taking off and landing
2.	Aircraft being towed
3.	Aircraft
4.	Vehicles

Converging aircraft: The aircraft on the right has right of way, **"On the right, in the right".** The aircraft giving way turns right to pass behind the other

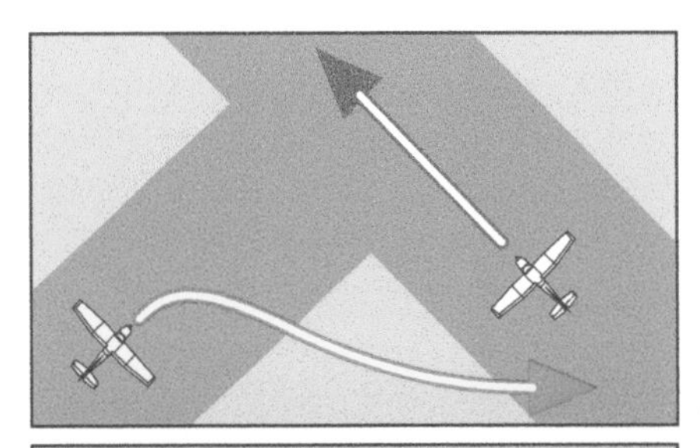

Head On: Both aircraft stop or turn to the right

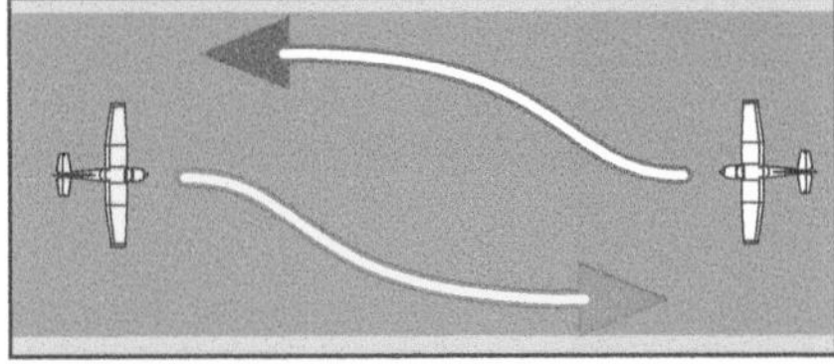

Overtaking The overtaking aircraft must keep well clear of the other aircraft.

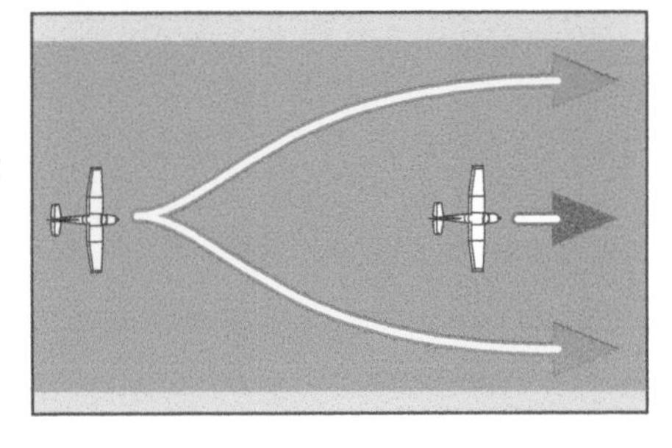

The **lights to be displayed** by flying machines at night are:

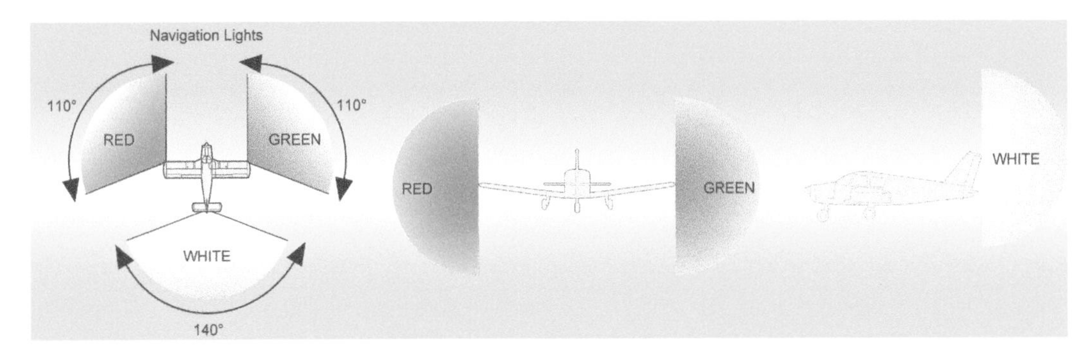

The **UK low flying** rules:

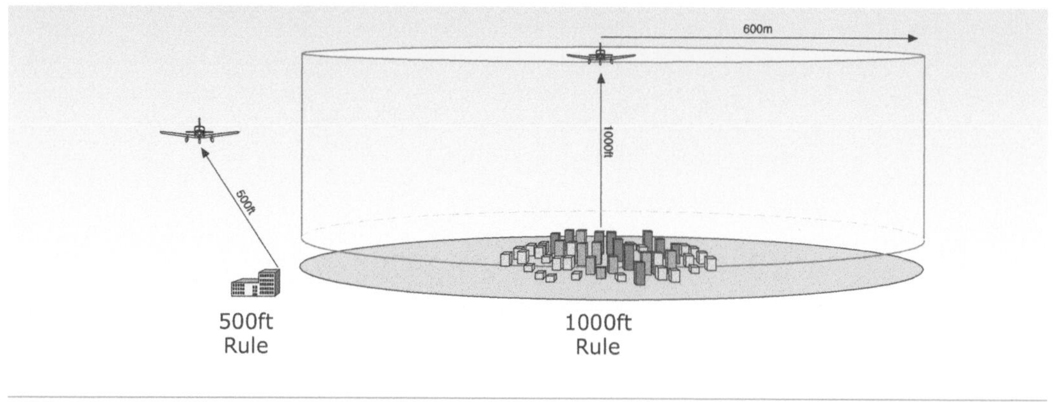

500ft Rule	Fly no closer than 500ft to any person, vessel, vehicle or structure, except when taking off and landing.
1000ft Rule	Fly no lower than 1000ft above the highest obstacle within a radius of 600m from the aircraft when over the congested areas of cities, towns or settlements, or over an open-air assembly of people.

Note: The UK low flying rules are different to the Standardised European Rules of the Air (SERA), and currently subject to an exemption. This may well change during the publishing cycle of this publication.

To fly in accordance with **Visual Flight Rules (VFR)** and aircraft must be in **Visual Meteorological Conditions (VMC)**. The UK VMC minima are:

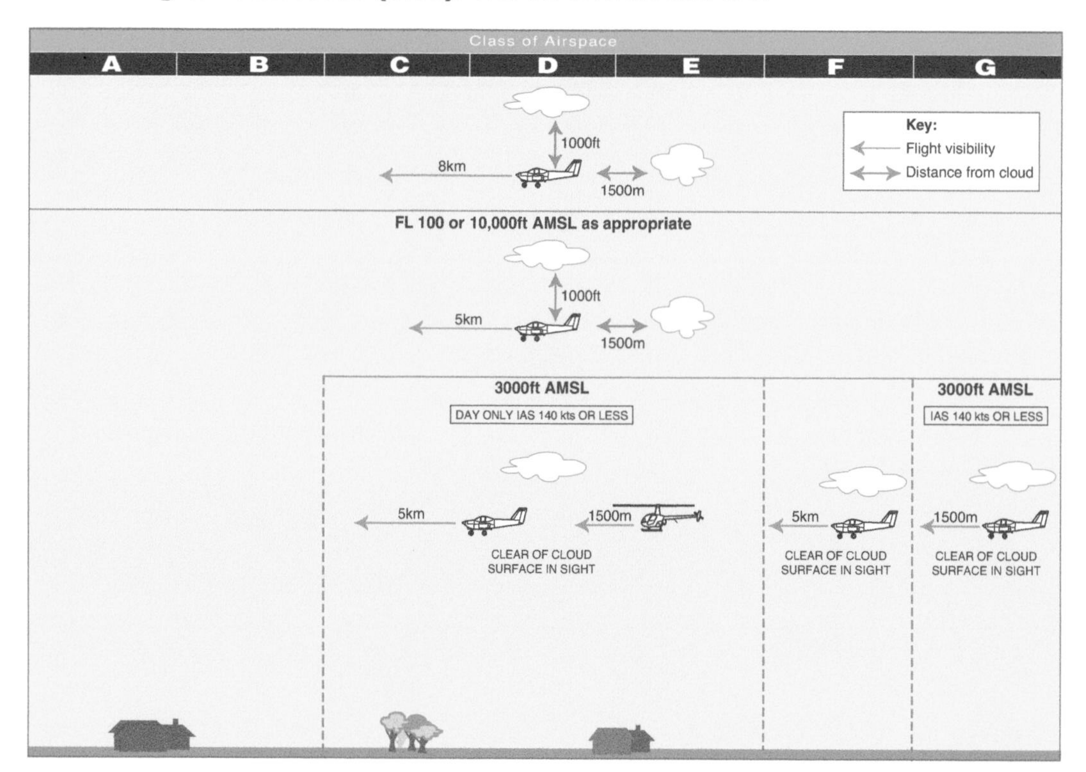

Note: The UK VMC minima are different to the Standardised European Rules of the Air (SERA) VMC minima, and currently subject to an exemption. This may well change during the publishing cycle of this publication

If weather conditions are below VMC minima then they are IMC - **Instrument Meteorological Conditions**. In IMC, an aircraft must fly in accordance with **Instrument Flight Rules** (IFR).

The following **ground-air visual signals** may be used:

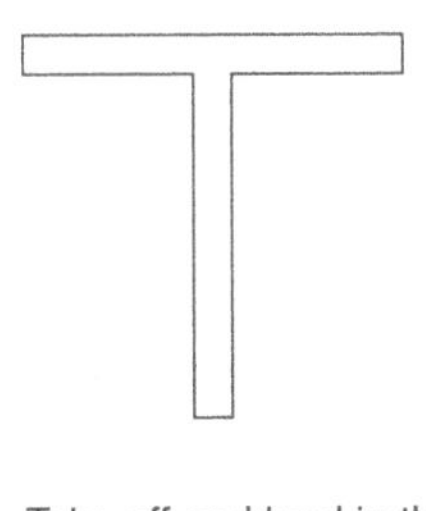

Take-off and land in the direction of the shaft of the T

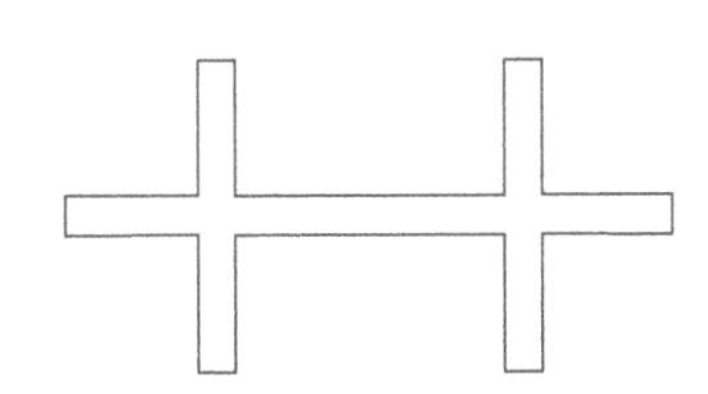

Gliding in progress

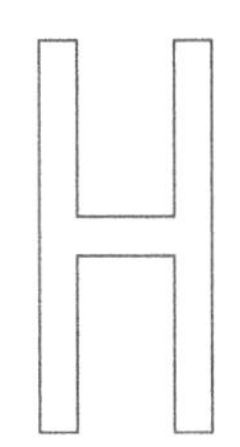

Helicopters may only land or take-off within the designated area

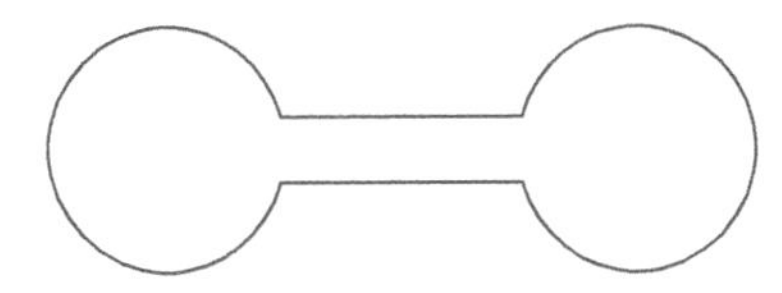

Aircraft are required to land, take off and taxi on runways and taxiways only

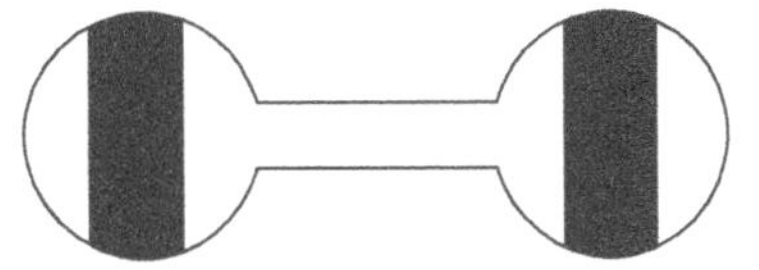

Aircraft are required to land and take off on runways only, but may taxi off runways and taxiways

Runway or taxiway (or a section) is unfit for the movement of aircraft

Right-hand circuit in force

Special precautions must be observed in approaching to land or in landing

Landing prohibited

Location of the air traffic services reporting office

Marshalling Signals

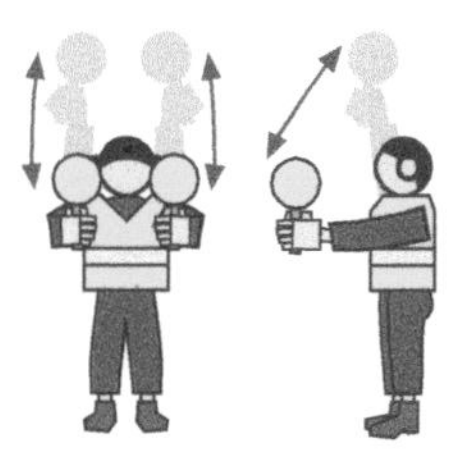
Identify Gate

Straight Ahead

Turn Left

Turn Right

Wingwalker

Proceed to next Marshaller

Start Engines

Cut Engines

Slow Down

Hold Position

Normal Stop

Emergency Stop

Set Brakes

Chocks inserted

Release Brakes

Chocks Removed

Affirmative/All Clear

Dispatch Aircraft

Negative

Fire

Pilot to Marshaller

Brakes Engaged

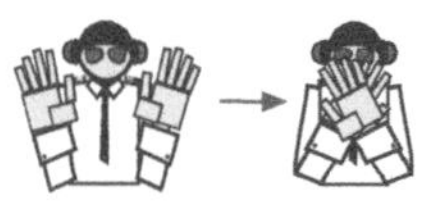
Insert Chocks

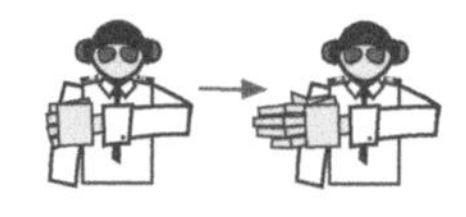
Brakes Released

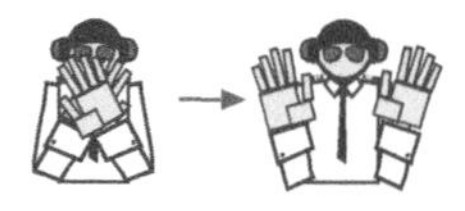
Remove Chocks

Helicopter Marshalling Signals

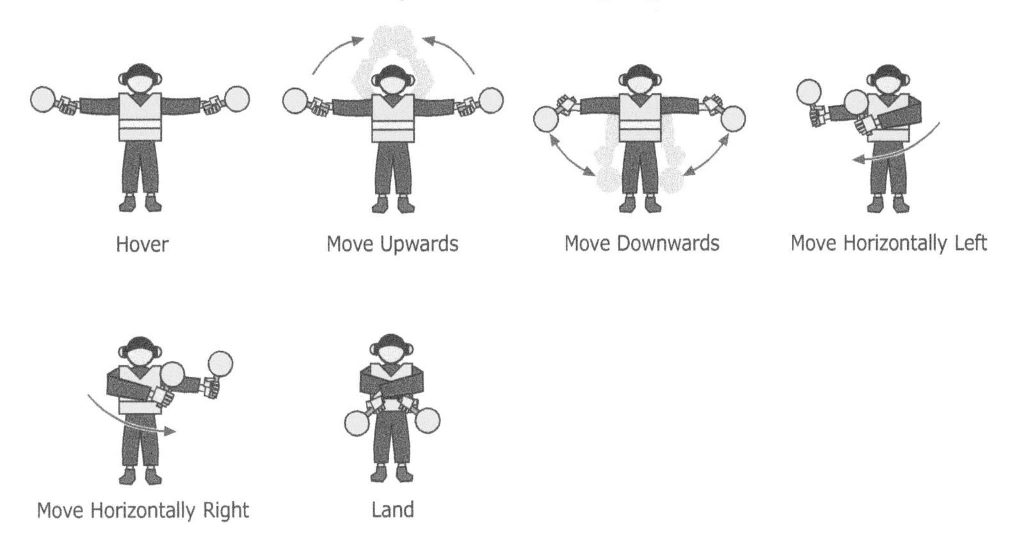

Light signals can be made from aircraft to ATSU and vice versa:

ATC Light Signals to Aircraft on Ground

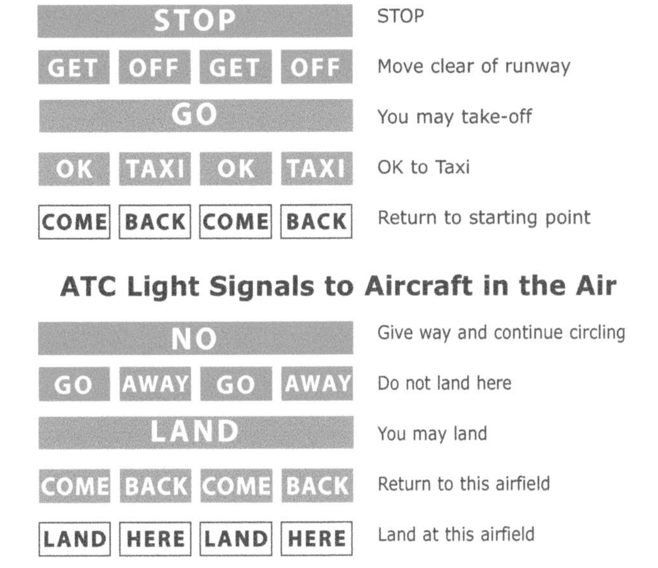

An aircraft which is **intercepted** by another aircraft must immediately:

- Follow the instructions given by the intercepting aircraft, interpreting and responding to visual signals if necessary;

- notify, if possible, the appropriate Air Traffic Services Unit;

- attempt to establish radio communication with the intercepting aircraft or with the appropriate intercept control unit by making a general call on the emergency frequency 121.500MHz, giving the identity of the intercepted aircraft and the nature of the flight;

- if equipped with SSR transponder, select Code 7700 and Mode C (ALT), unless otherwise instructed by the appropriate Air Traffic Services Unit.

Altimeter Setting Procedures

The **transition altitude** is the altitude above which the altimeter can be set to the Standard Setting (1013hPa) so that the altimeter indicates Flight Level.

The **transition level** is the lowest useable flight level above the transition altitude.

The **transition layer** is the layer between the transition altitude and transition level.

As a general rule, a VFR flight can use any desired altimeter setting, although when flying within or beneath controlled airspace such as a TMA or CTA, the QNH of an airfield under than TMA or CTA should be used. IFR flights usually use QNH when flying beneath the transition altitude, and Standard Setting (1013hPa) when flying above the transition altitude, except when descending from a Flight Level to an altitude.

Secondary Surveillance Radar (Transponder)

The Mode C (ALT) feature of a Transponder enables the transponder to transmit the aircraft's Pressure Altitude (that is, the aircraft's vertical level based on the 1013hPa setting, otherwise known as Flight Level).

The emergency transponder codes are:

7700 Distress
7600 Radio communications failure
7500 Unlawful interference

Air Traffic Management (annex 11)

The objectives of Air Traffic Services are to:

- Prevent collisions between aircraft
- Prevent collisions between aircraft on the manoeuvring area and obstructions on that area
- Expedite and maintain an orderly flow of air traffic
- Provide advice and information of the safe and efficient conduct of flights
- Notify organisations of aircraft in need of search and rescue aid, and assist such organisations

Air Traffic Control (ATC) definitions:

Aerodrome Control Service	- an air traffic control service for aerodrome traffic
Aerodrome Traffic	- all traffic on the manoeuvring area of an aerodrome and all aircraft flying in the vicinity of an aerodrome
Air Traffic	- all aircraft in flight or operating on the manoeuvring area of an aerodrome
Alerting service	- a service provided to notify appropriate organisations regarding aircraft in need of search and rescue aid, and assist such organisations as required
Approach Control Service	- an air traffic control service for arriving and departing controlled flights
Area Control Service	- an Air Traffic Control service for controlled flights in control areas
Flight Information Service	- a service provided for the purpose of giving advice and information useful for the safe and efficient conduct of flights
Radar approach	- an approach where the final approach phase is conducted under the direction of a radar controller
Radar vectoring	- the provision of navigational guidance to aircraft, in the form of specific headings, based on the use of radar

The following rules apply to flight in various **airspace classifications**:

controlled airspace = Classes A, B, C, D and E; **uncontrolled airspace** = Classes F and G.

Airspace Class	Flight Rules	Notes
Class A	IFR flight only	All flights subject to ATC service and separated from each other
Class B	IFR & VFR flight	All flights subject to ATC service and separated from each other
Class C	IFR & VFR flight	All flights subject to ATC service. IFR flights separated from all other flights. VFR flights separated from IFR flights and receive traffic information about other VFR flights
Class D	IFR & VFR flight	All flights subject to ATC service. IFR flights separated from all other IFR flights and receive traffic information about VFR flights. VFR flights receive traffic information about other flights
Class E	IFR & VFR flight	IFR flights subject to ATC service and separated from all other IFR flights. All flights receive traffic information as far as is practical
Class F	IFR & VFR flight	Participating IFR flights separated from other IFR flights and receive an air traffic advisory service as far as is practical. All flights receive flight information service if requested
Class G	IFR & VFR flight	All flights receive flight information service if requested

Aeronautical Information Service (annex 15)

The **Aeronautical Information Publication** (AIP) has three main sections:

GEN	General	Codes, tables and listings, air traffic, AIS and meteorological services, differences from ICAO procedures etc.
ENR	En-route	Rules and procedures, airspace etc.
AD	Aerodrome	General and specific aerodrome and heliport information

Aerodromes (annex 14)

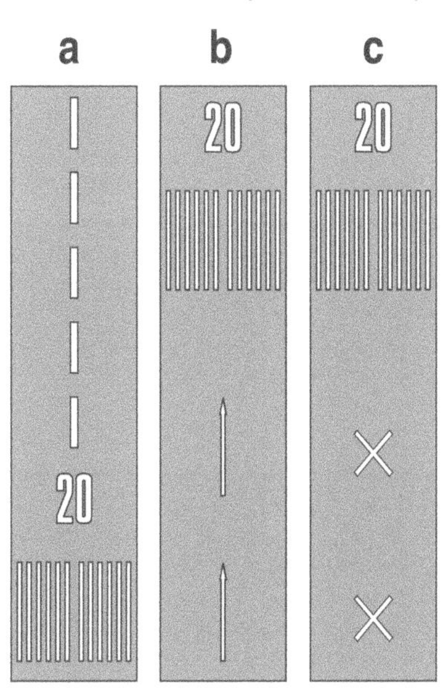

Runway markings are white

a Threshold, centre line and runway direction in tens of degrees magnetic

b A displaced threshold, the area of the arrows cannot be used for landing

c A displaced threshold, the area of the crosses is unfit for any movement of aircraft

There may be **runway lights** to mark the useable portion of the runway, green at the start end of the runway, red at the stop end.

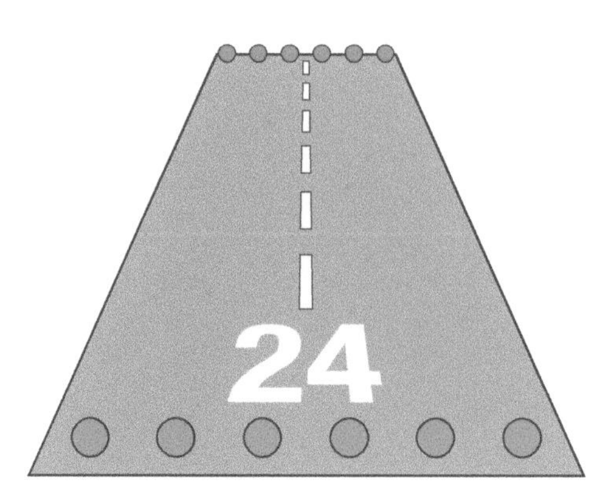

Taxiway markings are yellow:

Boundary Markers:

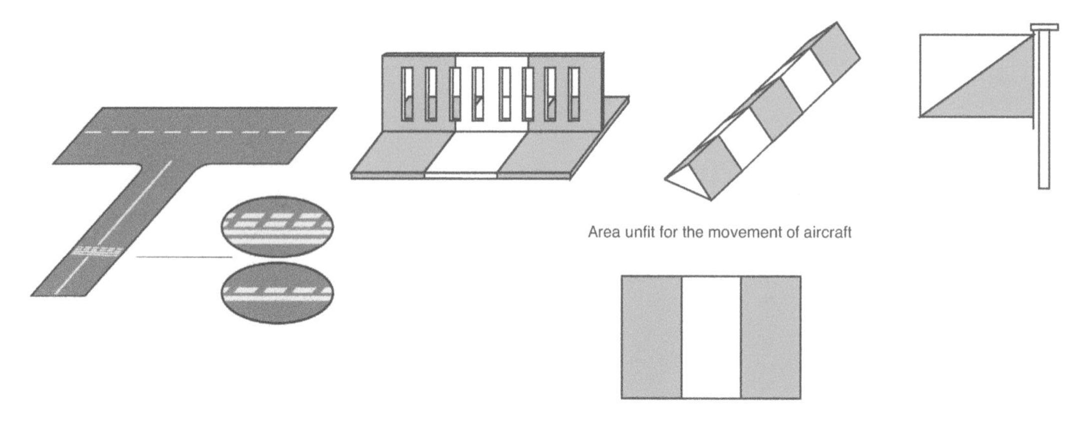

Taxiway signs giving information are usually coloured yellow and black. Mandatory taxiway signs have a red background

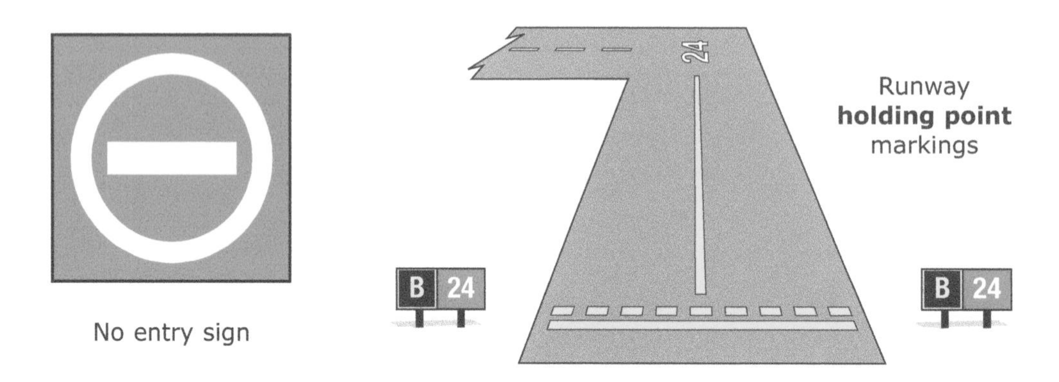

An aircraft must not move on the **apron or manoeuvring** area of an aerodrome without permission:

Aircraft stand – a designated area of an apron used for the parking of an aircraft.

Apron – the part of an aerodrome where aircraft can load and unload, refuel and park.

Landing area – the part of the movement area for the take-off or landing of aircraft.

Manoeuvring area – the part of the aerodrome provided for the take-off and landing and movement of aircraft, excluding the apron and any maintenance area.

Movement area – the part of an aerodrome used by aircraft taking-off, landing and taxying, including the apron (this is not the same as the manoeuvring area).

Search and Rescue (annex 12)

An aircraft that observes an aircraft or surface craft in distress must, first and foremost, keep it in sight for as long as necessary.

The following **search and rescue ground signals** may be made by survivors:

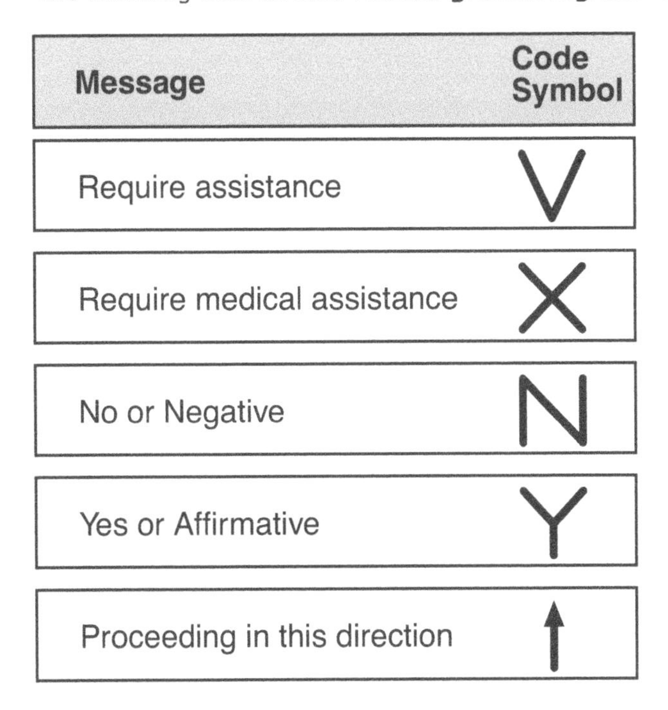

Message	Code Symbol
Require assistance	V
Require medical assistance	X
No or Negative	N
Yes or Affirmative	Y
Proceeding in this direction	↑

To acknowledge that it has understood these signals, and aircraft may rock its wings (by day) or switch the landing light on and off twice (by night).

Security (annex 17)

The primary objective of each contracting ICAO state is to safeguard passengers, ground personnel and flight crew, as well as the general public, against any acts of unlawful interference.

Each contracting state should have an organization that is responsible for organizing its practices, procedures and the development and implementation of regulations to safe guard against unlawful interference.

This organization:

- protects the safety of its crew both on the ground and in the air as well as safeguards the general public as well from acts of unlawful interference.
- is able to respond quickly to any increases in security threat.

Accident and Incident Investigation (annex 13)

ICAO definition**:** *The sole objective of the investigation of an accident or incident shall be the prevention of accidents and incidents. It is not the purpose of this activity to apportion blame or liability*.

An accident is an occurrence associated with the operation of an aircraft which takes place between the time any person boards the aircraft with the intention of flight until such time as all such persons have left the aircraft, in which:

1.) A person is fatally or seriously injured as a result of being in the aircraft, or by direct contact with any part of the aircraft, including parts which have become detached from the aircraft.

2.) The aircraft sustains damage or structural failure which adversely affects the structural strength, performance or flight characteristics of the aircraft, and would normally require major repair or replacement.

3.) The aircraft is missing or is completely inaccessible.

The 'State of Occurrence' must institute an investigation into the circumstances of an accident. The State of Occurrence is defined as the state in the territory of which an accident or incident occurs.

National Law

UK airspace contains **Prohibited, Restricted and Danger Areas**. These areas are designated using the following protocol:

Nationality Letters These are the letters assigned to the state or territory, and are the same is the first two letters of an ICAO aerodrome code. In the case of the UK the location indicator letters are EG.

P, R or D To indicate Prohibited, Restricted or Danger Area.

Figures The individual number for the area.

Thus, UK danger area 006 is full identified as: EG D006.

Where depicted on charts, the area designator is followed by a forward slash and then a two digit number which indicates the ceiling of the area in thousands of feet amsl. Thus a figure of 2.9 indicates a ceiling of 2,900ft amsl.

In the UK, '**night**' is defined as the period from 30 minutes after sunset to 30 minutes before sunrise.

Where used, an **airfield beacon** at a UK airfield flashes a two letter morse code identifier in green (for a civilian airfield) or red (for a military airfield).

En-route **obstacles** which exceed 300ft agl will be lit, normally by a steady red light(s). An exceptionally tall obstacle may be lit by high-intensity lights which flash white (strobes).

EASA Private Pilot Licence & Light Aircraft Pilot Licence Aeroplane & Helicopter Air Law

Time allowed: 35 minutes

No. of questions: 16

Total Marks: 100

Instructions:

- The paper consists of 16 multiple choice questions. The pass mark is 75% (ie 12 questions or more must be answered correctly). Marks are not deducted for incorrect answers.
- Be sure to carefully read each question and ensure that you understand it before considering the answer choices. Only one of the answers is complete and correct; the others are either incomplete, incorrect or based on a misconception.
- You should indicate the correct answer by placing a cross in the appropriate box of the answer sheet. If you decide to change an answer, you should erase the original choice and put a cross in the box representing your new selection.
- Each question has an average answer time of just over 2 minutes. No credit is given for unanswered questions.

Air Law Practice Paper ONE

1. The Transition Altitude at a specific airfield is:

(a) Dependant on pressure setting

(b) Listed in the Aeronautical Information Publication (AIP)

(c) Always 18,000ft

(d) Always 3,000ft

2. A Class 2 medical certificate has the following period of validity:

(a) 50 months until the holder is 50 years old

(b) 60 months until the holder is 40 years old

(c) 60 months until the holder is 60 years old

(d) 50 months until the holder is 40 years old

3. The person responsible for the operation and safety of an aircraft during flight is:

(a) The Air Traffic Controller

(b) The aircraft operator

(c) The pilot operating the flight controls at any given moment

(d) The pilot-in-command

4. Which of the following statements is true in relation to Class D airspace?

(a) VFR flights receive traffic information about other VFR flights

(b) VFR flights are separated from IFR flights

(c) IFR flights are not permitted

(d) VFR flights are not permitted

5. A line of red lights across the runway width indicates:

(a) A displaced threshold

(b) An exit

(c) The 'stop' end of the runway

(d) That the runway is unavailable for use

6. If a pilot suffers a significant incapacitating injury, the pilot's medical certificate:

(a) Must be considered as suspended, subject to arrangements made by the authority

(b) Should be considered as suspended, the holder may 'self-certify' when fit

(c) Should be considered as valid unless the authority states otherwise

(d) Is permanently invalidated

7. An aeroplane or helicopter pilot intends to make a flight carrying passengers; which of the following statements is correct?

(a) The pilot must then complete 3 take-offs and 3 landings within the next 90 days in an aircraft of the same class or type

(b) The pilot must have made 3 take-offs or 3 landings with an instructor in the preceding 90 days in an aircraft of any class or type

(c) The pilot must have made 3 take-offs and 3 landings as sole manipulator of the controls in the preceding 90 days in an aircraft of the same class or type

(d) The pilot must have made 3 take-offs and 3 landings as sole manipulator of the controls in the preceding 90 days in an aircraft of any class or type

8. In order to operate an aircraft radio over the territory of another state:

(a) Both the radio and the radio operator must be licenced by the state over whose territory the aircraft is being flown

(b) The radio (but not the radio operator) must be licenced by the state over whose territory the aircraft is being flown

(c) The radio (but not the radio operator) must be licenced by the state of registry of the aircraft

(d) The radio and the radio operator must be licenced by the state of registry of the aircraft

9. Which of the following does NOT invalidate a Certificate of Airworthiness?

(a) An unauthorised repair or modification

(b) Change of ownership not notified within 7 days

(c) Operating outside the limits stated on placards in the cockpit

(d) Use of a material not approved by the CAA

10. In relation to aircraft of different classes converging in flight, which of the following statements is true?

(a) Gliders (sailplanes) must give way to airships and balloons

(b) Balloons must give way to airships

(c) Airships must give way to gliders (sailplanes) and balloons

(d) Gliders (sailplanes) must give way to aircraft towing other aircraft

11. A white T in the signal area of an aerodrome means:

(a) Aeroplanes and gliders (sailplanes) taking off or landing must do so parallel to the shaft of the T and towards the cross arm

(b) The aerodrome has technical facilities for aircraft engineering

(c) Approach and take off is particularly susceptible to turbulence

(d) Direction of take-off and landing may differ

12. The transition level is defined as:

(a) The altitude above which the altimeter can be set to the Standard Setting (1013hPa)

(b) The Flight Level below which the altimeter can be set to the Standard Setting (1013hPa)

(c) The layer between the transition altitude and transition level

(d) The lowest available Flight Level above the transition altitude

13. With regard to an aircraft's Certificate of Registration:

(a) It is not required for aircraft of less than 5700kg MTWA

(b) It need not show the name and address of the registered owner

(c) By ICAO recommendation it should be carried on all flights

(d) It contains the limitations of the Flight Manual / Pilot's Operating Handbook

14. In relation to ground markings painted on runways and taxiways, ICAO recommend that:

(a) Runway and taxiway markings should be white

(b) Runway markings should be yellow and taxiway markings should be white

(c) Runway markings should be white and taxiway markings should be yellow

(d) Runway and taxiway markings should be yellow

15. When take-offs and landings are not confined to a runway, the commander of an aeroplane that is taking off shall position:

(a) To the right of an aircraft ahead, leaving it clear to the left

(b) To the left of an aircraft ahead, leaving it clear to the right

(c) Directly behind the aircraft ahead

(d) Either side, at the following pilot's discretion

16. In the UK, the period from 30 minutes after sunset to 30 minutes before sunrise at the surface is defined as:

(a) Surface twilight

(b) Civil Twilight

(c) Day

(d) Night

1. The period of validity of a medical certificate:

(a) Starts from the end of the month in which the medical certificate was issued

(b) Must be no longer than the period of validity of the pilot's licence

(c) Can be extended by up to 20% by arrangement with an AME

(d) Starts from the date of the medical examination

2. In relation to the Rules of the Air:

(a) A pilot-in-command may deviate from the rules if absolutely necessary for safety reasons

(b) A pilot can deviate from the rules of the air for operational reasons

(c) No deviation from the rules of the air is permitted under any circumstances

(d) Deviation from the rules of the air requires ATC clearance

3. According to the Chicago Convention (Convention on International Civil Aviation), which of the following are required to be carried on an international flight?

(a) Certificate of Airworthiness; Certificate of Registration and invoices for all fuel on board

(b) Certificate of Airworthiness and Certificate of Registration

(c) Crew logbooks and passports

(d) Journey logbook, crew licences and noise certificate

4. An aeroplane is flying at 3500ft amsl in Class E airspace. In order to comply with VMC minima, the minimum required conditions are:

(a) 5km flight visibility, 1500m horizontally and 1000ft vertically clear of cloud

(b) 1·5nm flight visibility, clear of cloud, in sight of the surface

(c) 5km flight visibility, clear of cloud

(d) 1500m flight visibility, clear of cloud and in sight of the surface

5. In an overtaking situation involving aeroplanes:

(a) The overtaking aeroplane has right of way

(b) The aeroplane being overtaken has right of way

(c) The aeroplane being overtaken must maintain course and speed

(d) The aeroplane being overtaken must descend

6. The basic privileges of a Private Pilot Licence (PPL) holder include the right to:

(a) Fly for either business or leisure, with appropriate remuneration

(b) Fly any aircraft for which a rating is held for any purpose

(c) Fly without remuneration on non-commercial operations

(d) Fly as co-pilot on commercial operations

7. The holder of a medical certificate must seek advice from the authority or an Authorised Medical Examiner (AME) without delay if:

(a) They become aware of the need for a surgical operation

(b) They decide to become a blood or bone marrow donor

(c) They make any out-patient appointment with a hospital or clinic

(d) They contract an illness that reduces their fitness to fly

8. The apron and part of the airfield used for take-off, landing and taxying, is known as:

(a) The mandatory area

(b) The manoeuvring area

(c) The movement area

(d) The aircraft stand

9. According to ICAO annex six, and subject to any additional equipment prescribed by the relevant authority, the minimum aircraft instrumentation for VFR flight is best represented by which of the following options?

(i) A magnetic compass.

(ii) An accurate timepiece.

(iii) A sensitive pressure altimeter.

(iv) An airspeed indicator

(v) An attitude indicator

(vi) A turn coordinator

(a) (i), (ii) and (vi)

(b) (i), (ii), (iii) and (iv)

(c) (i), (iii), (iv) and (v)

(d) (i), (iv), (v) and (vi)

10. The Secondary Surveillance Radar (SSR) transponder code 7700 is used to indicate:

(a) An aircraft carrying out aerobatics

(b) A communications failure

(c) A practice or real emergency

(d) An emergency

11. A ground-to-air Search and Rescue signal by survivors in the form of a single arrow, has the meaning:

(a) This is North

(b) Aircraft wreckage in this direction

(c) Proceeding in this direction

(d) What is in this direction?

12. An aircraft is approaching another aircraft 'head on' and there is a danger of collision. The appropriate response is which of the following?

(a) The smaller aircraft should alter course to the right

(b) Each aircraft must alter course to the right

(c) Each aircraft should alter course to the left (if on the ground)

(d) The larger aircraft should start a maximum rate descent

13. An aircraft that has been intercepted should attempt to contact the intercepting aircraft on which radio frequency?

(a) The radio frequency currently in use

(b) The 'FIS' frequency for the FIR within which the aircraft are flying

(c) The VHF emergency frequency - 121.5MHz

(d) The frequency of the closest military airfield

14. Runway markings are normally painted in:

(a) Solid white colour

(b) A yellow outline only

(c) Solid green colour

(d) Red

15. In flight by night you see only the red navigation light of another aircraft flying at approximately the same level as your aircraft, and on a constant relative bearing of 060°:

(a) There is no collision risk

(b) There is a collision risk, you should avoid passing over, under or ahead of the other aircraft. Prepare to alter course to right to pass behind the other aircraft

(c) You have right of way. Maintain course and speed but be prepared to take avoiding action

(d) Increase speed to pass ahead of the other aircraft. As you are overtaking, you have right of way

16. A 'reportable' accident, as defined by ICAO, has occurred if:

(a) A person is killed on board an aircraft at any time

(b) A part falling from an aircraft seriously injures a person on the ground

(c) The commander of the aircraft becomes ill

(d) An aircraft is damaged whilst being positioned for maintenance within a hangar

Air Law Practice Paper THREE

1. Signs on an aerodrome which are predominantly yellow and black are:

(a) Information signs (for example, taxiway directions)

(b) Apron designators only

(c) Mandatory signs (for example, 'No Entry')

(d) Aerodrome boundary markers

2. A pilot engaged in international air navigation:

(a) Must hold a licence validated by the state to be visited or over-flown

(b) Must hold a licence issued or validated by the state in which the aircraft is registered

(c) Must seek approval for the flight from the national licensing authority

(d) Must hold a JAR licence

3. The transponder code '7500' can be used to indicate:

(a) General conspicuity

(b) Radio communications failure

(c) Unlawful interference

(d) Aircraft performing aerobatics

Paper THREE

4. Consider the following statement:

The sole objective of .... shall be the prevention of accidents and incidents. It is not the purpose of this activity to apportion blame or liability.

The missing words are:

(a) the Competent Authority

(b) ICAO

(c) the investigation of an accident or incident

(d) EASA

5. The vertical level of an aircraft approaching or departing from an airfield should normally be expressed as:

(a) Flight Level at or below the Transition Altitude

(b) Altitude at or below the Transition Altitude

(c) Flight Level only when at the Transition Level

(d) Flight Level only above 10,000ft

6. By ICAO definition, within class D airspace:

(a) IFR flights are separated from other IFR and VFR flights

(b) IFR flights are separated from other IFR flights and are given information about VFR flights

(c) VFR flights are separated from other VFR and IFR flights

(d) Only IFR flight is permitted

7. Choose which of the following combinations best describes the objectives of Air Traffic Services as defined by ICAO:

[i] Prevent collisions between aircraft

[ii] Prevent collisions between aircraft on the manoeuvring area and obstructions on that area

[iii] Expedite and maintain an orderly flow of air traffic

[iv] Provide advice and information of the safe and efficient conduct of flights

[v] Notify organisations of aircraft in need of search and rescue aid, and assist such organisations

(a) [i], [ii] and [v]

(b) [ii], [iii] and [iv]

(c) [i], [ii] and [iv]

(d) [i], [ii], [iii], [iv] and [v]

8. If a Pilot In Command is given an ATC clearance that the PIC considers is unsuitable, the PIC should:

(a) Carry-out the clearance and file a report on landing

(b) Amend the clearance as necessary on reading it back to ATC

(c) Request and try to obtain an amended clearance

(d) Disregard the clearance

9. The transponder code 7600 indicates:

(a) A radio communications failure

(b) That the aircraft is performing aerobatics

(c) The VFR conspicuity code

(d) The aerobatics conspicuity code

10. Flight time to be credited for the grant of a licence or rating should be flown:

(a) In the same category of aircraft for which the licence or rating is sought

(b) In any aircraft holding a certificate of airworthiness

(c) Always with a qualified instructor on board

(d) In any aircraft defined as a flying machine

11. An area of runway that is unfit for the movement of aircraft may be marked by:

(a) Red crosses painted on the surface

(b) Yellow 'ladder' markings across the taxiway or runway

(c) Two continuous and broken lines across the taxiway or runway

(d) Two or more white crosses painted onto the surface of the runway

12. A continuous red light directed to an aircraft on the ground means:

(a) Return to your starting point on the airfield

(b) Stop

(c) Stop until conflicting traffic has passed

(d) Give way to traffic merging, then continue

13. Before carrying out a flight by day on which it is planned to carry passengers, a pilot must ensure that:

(a) 3 take-offs and landings have been completed as sole manipulator of the controls of any aircraft in the preceding 90 days

(b) A 'club' check ride has been undertaken

(c) 3 take-offs and landings as sole manipulator of the controls in the same type or class of aircraft have been completed in the preceding 90 days

(d) 1 take-off and 1 landing have been made in the preceding 90 days under the supervision of a flight instructor

14. A ground air visual signal in the shape of the letter V means:

(a) Assistance is required

(b) Medical assistance is required

(c) Proceed in the direction indicated by the point of the V

(d) There are five survivors

15. The Mode C feature of an aircraft's transponder:

(a) Will transmit the aircraft's flight level to ATC

(b) Is selected by ATC by remote control

(c) Is selected using the 'STBY' or 'SBY' control

(d) Displays the aircraft's heading to ATC

16. Where two aircraft of the same class are converging in flight, the aircraft that has the right of way must:

(a) Orbit to its right immediately

(b) Maintain its height and reduce speed

(c) Maintain its height and speed

(d) Maintain its heading and speed

Air Law paper 1 Q1 Answer B

The Transition Altitude may vary at different airfields and in different classes of airspace. The Transition Altitude for a UK airfield is listed in the AD (Aerodrome) section of the UK Aeronautical Information Publication (AIP).

Further Reference: PPL2 Air Law>Rules of the Air and Air Traffic Services>Transition Level

Air Law paper 1 Q2 Answer B

A class two medical certificate issued under 'PART-Med' has the following periods of validity:

Age	Period of validity
Up to 40	60 months*
40 - 49	24 months**
50 and over	12 months

* not valid after 42nd birthday

** not valid after 51st birthday

All periods of validity run from medical date, to the exact anniversary of that date; for example if a certificate is issued on 14 June, the validity will run to the 14th day of the appropriate month.

Further Reference: PPL2 Air Law>JAA/EASA Regulations>JAA Regulations General

Air Law paper 1 Q3 Answer D

It can't be said enough times - it is the Pilot In Command (PIC) who is ultimately responsible for the safe operation of an aircraft in flight - and this responsibility extends from the pre-flight actions (such as flight planning, loading and checking of the aircraft) all the way through to when the last of the passengers and crew have left the aircraft at the end of the flight and all the paperwork has been completed.

Further Reference: PPL2 Operational Procedures>Operation of Aircraft>Operation of Aircraft

Air Law paper 1 Q4 Answer A

Within Class D airspace:

- All flights are subject to ATC service
- IFR flights are separated from other IFR flights
- IFR flights receive traffic information about VFR flights
- VFR flights receive traffic information about other VFR flights

Further Reference: PPL2 Air Law>Rules of the Air and Air Traffic Services>Area Control Service

Air Law paper 1 Q5 Answer C

Runway 'end' lights are as shown in the diagram below:

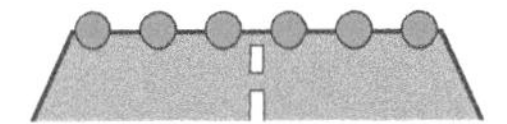

Further Reference: PPL2 Air Law>Rules of the Air>Aerodrome Lighting

Air Law paper 1 Q6 Answer A

In the case of illness exceeding 21 days or more, or injury, either of which involves incapacity to undertake flight crew functions, or pregnancy, a pilot's medical certificate is deemed to be suspended upon the occurrence of such injury or the expiry of such period of illness or the confirmation of the pregnancy, and remains suspended subject to arrangements made by the competent authority.

Further Reference: PPL2 Air Law>JAA/EASA Regulations>JAA Regulations - General

Air Law paper 1 Q7 Answer C

An aeroplane or helicopter pilot must not fly as pilot in command of an aircraft carrying passengers unless within the preceding 90 days he or she has made three take-offs and three landings as the sole manipulator of the controls of an aircraft of the same type or class. If the flight is to be carried out at night and his or her licence does not include an instrument rating, at least one of those take-offs and landings must have been at night.

Further Reference: PPL2 Air Law>JAA/EASA Regulations>Private Pilot Licence (Aeroplane) - PPL(A)

Air Law paper 1 Q8 Answer D

Article 30 of the Convention on International Civil Aviation (also known as the Chicago Convention) deals with aircraft radio equipment. According to article 30, aircraft of a state flying in or over the territory of another state shall only carry radios licensed and used in accordance with the regulations of the state in which the aircraft is registered. The radio(s) may only be used by members of the flight crew suitably licenced by the state in which the aircraft is registered.

Further Reference: PPL2 Air Law>Legislation>Basis of Aviation Law

Air Law paper 1 Q9 Answer B

A Certificate of Airworthiness will cease to be in force if the aircraft, or such of its equipment as is necessary for the airworthiness of the aircraft, is overhauled, repaired or modified, or if any part of the aircraft or of such equipment is removed or is replaced, otherwise than in a manner and with material of a type approved by the Competent Authority either generally or in relation to a class of aircraft or to the particular aircraft.

Certain of the operating limits contained in the approved Pilot's Operating Handbook / Flight Manual (which forms part of the Certificate of Airworthiness) may be displayed in the cockpit in the form of placards - usually those relating to limiting airspeeds. Operating outside these limits invalidates the Certificate of Airworthiness. Failure to notify a change of ownership is an offence in relation to the Certificate of Registration, but not the Certificate of Airworthiness.

Further Reference: PPL2 Air Law>PPL2 Air Law>Airworthiness of Aircraft>Airworthiness of Aircraft *and* Aircraft Limits and Information

Air Law paper 1 Q10 Answer C

The Rules of the Air deals with the order of precedence, which is:

- flying machines must give way to airships, gliders (sailplanes) and balloons;
- airships must give way to gliders (sailplanes) and balloons;
- gliders (sailplanes) must give way to balloons;
- mechanically-driven aircraft must give way to aircraft which are towing other aircraft or objects.

Further Reference: PPL2 Air Law>Rules of the Air>Rights of Way in Flight

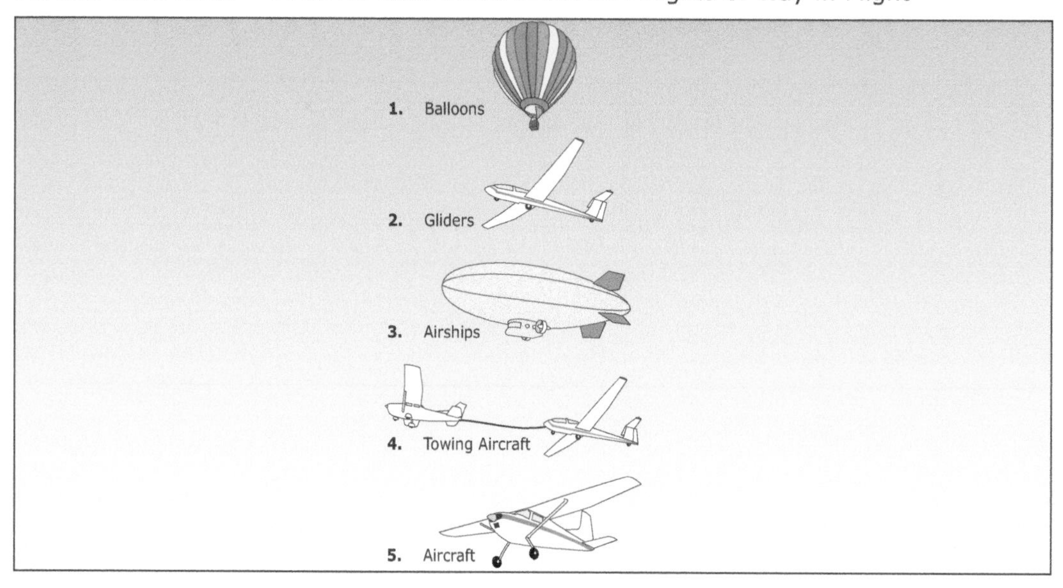

Air Law paper 1 Q11 Answer A

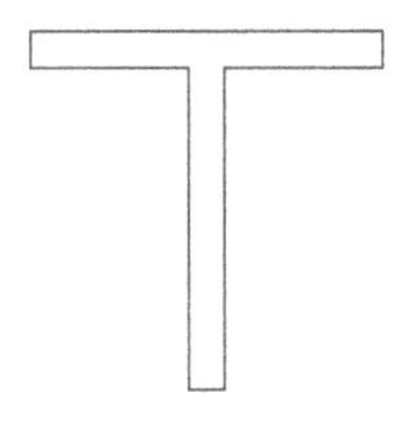

Take-off and land in the direction of the shaft of the T

Certain ground to air visual signals may be displayed at airfields which accept non-radio aircraft.

Further reference: PPL2 Air Law>Rules of the Air> Ground-to-Air Visual Signals

Air Law paper 1 Q12 Answer D

In terms of the 'changeover' between reporting altitude and reporting Flight Level, the following definitions apply:

Transition altitude	The altitude above which the altimeter can be set to Standard Setting (1013hPa) to read Flight Levels.
Transition level	The lowest Flight Level available for use above the transition altitude.
Transition layer	The layer between the transition altitude and the transition level.

Further Reference: PPL2 Air Law>Rules of the Air and Air Traffic Services>Transition Level

Air Law paper 1 Q13 Answer C

ICAO annex 7 (Aircraft Nationality and Registration Marks) recommends that the Certificate of Registration should be carried in the aircraft at all times.

Further Reference: PPL2 Air Law>Aircraft Registration>Aircraft Registration

Air Law paper 1 Q14 Answer C

ICAO annex 14 (Aerodromes) states that runway markings shall be white and taxiway and aircraft stand markings shall be yellow.

Further Reference PPL2 Air Law>Rules of the Air>Runways *and* Taxiway Signals and Markings

Air Law paper 1 Q15 Answer A

Where take-offs and landings are not confined to a runway:

- a flying machine or glider when landing shall leave clear on its left any aircraft which has landed or is already landing or about to take off;

- if such a flying machine or glider is about to turn it shall turn to the left after the commander of the aircraft has satisfied himself that such action will not interfere with other traffic movements;

- a flying machine about to take-off shall take up position and manoeuvre in such a way as to leave clear on its left any aircraft which has already taken off or is about to take-off.

Further Reference: PPL2 Air Law>Rules of the Air>Landing and Take-off

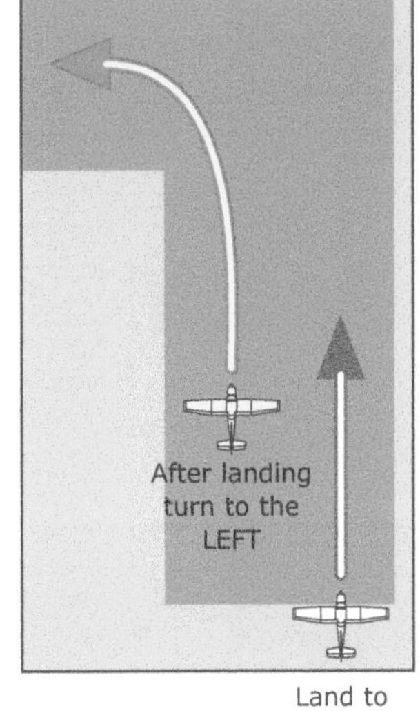

Land to the RIGHT

Air Law paper 1 Q16 Answer D

Under UK legislation, 'Night' is defined as the time from half an hour after sunset until half an hour before sunrise (both times inclusive), sunset and sunrise being determined at surface level.

Further Reference: PPL2 Air Law>JAA/EASA Regulations>Private Pilot Licence (Aeroplane)

Air Law paper 2 Q1 Answer D

The period of validity of a medical certificate begins on the date of the medical examination, the medical certificate itself is usually issued using the date of the medical examination. The period of validity runs to the exact anniversary day - for example a medical certificate issued on the 24th of April with a validity period of one year, runs until the 24th April on the next year.

Further reference: PPL2 Air Law>JAA/EASA Regulation>JAA Regulations General

Air Law paper 2 Q2 Answer A

The pilot-in-command (whether or not he or she is actually flying the aircraft) may depart from the rules of the air in circumstances that make such action absolutely necessary in the interests of safety.

Further reference: PPL2 Air Law>Rules of the Air> The Rules of the Air -General

Air Law paper 2 Q3 Answer B

Article 29 of the Convention on International Civil Aviation (also known as the Chicago Convention) states that before an international flight, the pilot in command must ensure that the aircraft is airworthy, duly registered and that the relevant documents are on board the aircraft. The required documents are:

Its Certificate of Registration

Its Certificate of Airworthiness

Crew licences

Journey logbook

Radio licence

A list of passenger names, places of embarkation and destination

A cargo manifest

Further Reference: PPL2 Air Law>Legislation>Basis of Aviation Law

Air Law paper 2 Q4 Answer A

The UK VMC minima are summarised at the table below. These minima must be learnt for all classes of airspace.

Further reference: PPL2 Air Law>Division of Airspace and Air Traffic Services> Visual Meteorological Conditions (VMC) and Instrument Meteorological Conditions (IMC)

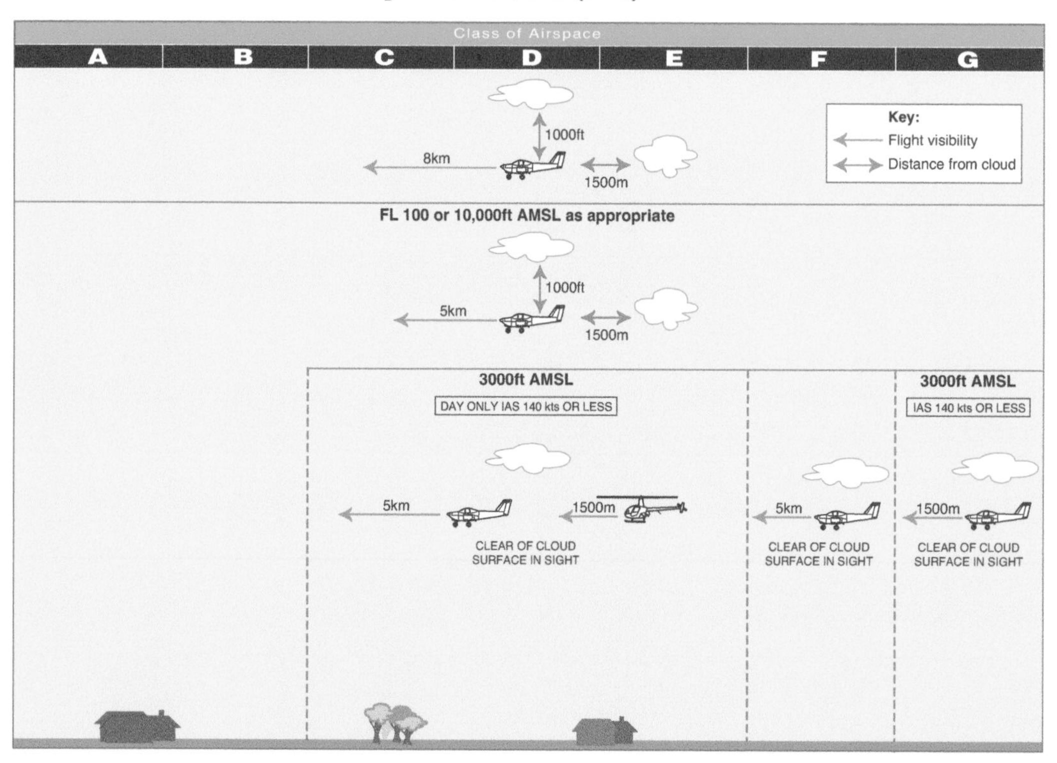

Air Law paper 2 Q5 Answer B

An aeroplane that is being overtaken by another aeroplane in flight has the right-of-way and the overtaking aeroplane, whether climbing, descending or in horizontal flight, must keep out of the way of the other aeroplane by altering its heading to the right. No subsequent change in the relative positions of the two aeroplanes absolves the overtaking aeroplane from this obligation until it is entirely past and clear.

Further reference: PPL2 Air Law>Rules of the Air> Rights of Way in Flight

Air Law paper 2 Q6 Answer C

The basic privilege of the holder of a Private Pilot Licence (PPL) is to act without remuneration as PIC or co-pilot on aeroplanes, helicopters or Touring Motor Gliders (as appropriate) engaged in non-commercial operations.

Further reference: PPL2 Air Law>JAA/EASA Regulations> Private Pilot Licence (Aeroplane)

Air Law paper 2 Q7 Answer A

Holders of medical certificates must, without undue delay, seek the advice of the authority or an AME when becoming aware of:

(1) hospital or clinic admission for more than 12 hours; or
(2) surgical operation or invasive procedure; or
(3) the regular use of medication; or
(4) the need for regular use of correcting lenses.

Further reference: PPL2 Air Law>JAA/EASA Regulations>JAA Requirements - General

Air Law paper 2 Q8 Answer C

ICAO annex 14 (Aerodromes) contains the following definition:

Movement Area - that part of an aerodrome to be used for the take-off, landing and taxying of aircraft, consisting of the manoeuvring area and the apron.

The apron and manoeuvring area are defined as follows:

Apron - the part of an aerodrome where aircraft can be stationed for the embarkation and disembarkation of passengers, for loading and unloading cargo, fuelling, maintenance and parking.

Manoeuvring area - the part of the aerodrome provided for the take-off and landing and movement of aircraft, excluding the apron and any maintenance area.

Further Reference: PPL2 Air Law>Rules of the Air>Movements at Aerodromes

Air Law paper 2 Q9 Answer B

ICAO annex six sets out recommended minimum equipment for aircraft, including instrumentation. According to annex six aircraft on a VFR flight should be equipped with at least:

A magnetic compass.
An accurate timepiece.
A sensitive pressure altimeter.
An airspeed indicator.
Any additional instrument prescribed by the relevant authority.

Further Reference: PPL2 Air Law>Operation of Aircraft>Instruments and Equipment

Air Law paper 2 Q10 Answer D

The standard emergency transponder codes are as follows:

- 7700 Distress
- 7600 Radio communications failure
- 7500 Unlawful interference

Further Reference: PPL2 Air Law>Rules of the Air>Distress, Difficulty and Urgency Signals

Air Law paper 2 Q11 Answer C

The Ground-Air visual signal code for use by survivors is set out below:

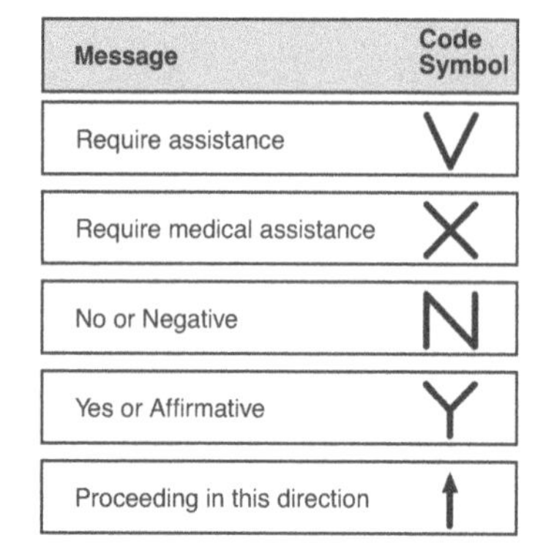

Message	Code Symbol
Require assistance	V
Require medical assistance	X
No or Negative	N
Yes or Affirmative	Y
Proceeding in this direction	↑

Further Reference: PPL2 Air Law>Search and Rescue>Search and Rescue Signals

Air Law paper 2 Q12 Answer B

Where two aircraft are converging 'head on', and there is a risk of collision, each must alter heading to the right.

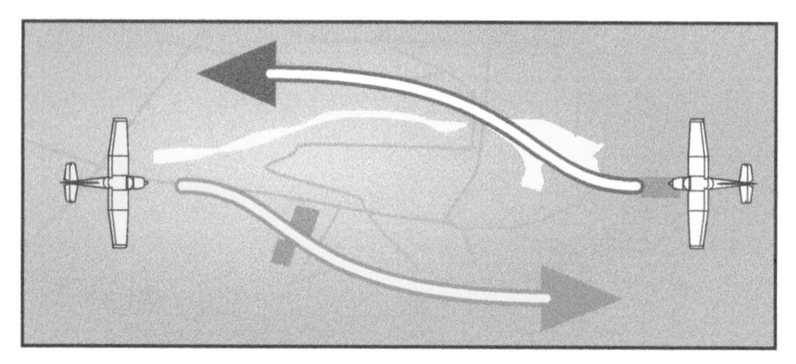

Further Reference: PPL2 Air Law>Rules of the Air>Rights of Way in Flight and Rights of Way on the Ground

Air Law paper 2 Q13 Answer C

The following initial actions are recommended to the pilot of an aircraft which has been intercepted:

1) Stay calm and comply immediately with the instructions or signals of the intercepting aircraft.
2) Notify the ATSU with which you are in contact.
3) Attempt to establish communication with the interceptor on the emergency frequency of 121.5, giving call sign and flight details.
4) Set the distress code - 7700 Mode C - on the transponder, unless instructed otherwise by an ATSU.

Further Reference: PPL2 Air Law>Rules of the Air>Interception of Aircraft

Air Law paper 2 Q14 Answer A

ICAO annex 14 (Aerodromes) states that runway markings shall be solid white, although this white may be outlined in black for clarity. Taxiway markings are usually yellow.

Further Reference: PPL2 Air Law>Rules of the Air>Runways

Air Law paper 2 Q15 Answer B

The question assumes that both the aircraft are 'flying machines' - that is heavier-than-air, power-driven aircraft. The fact that you can see a red light infers that it is on the port (left) wingtip of the other flying machine, and the relative bearing of the other flying machine puts it on your right-hand side - therefore it has right of way (*"**on the right, in the right**"*). Further, the fact that the bearing is constant means that the aircraft are almost certainly converging and there is a risk of a collision. Therefore you should avoid passing over, under or ahead of the other machine, and prepare to alter course to starboard (right) to pass clear behind it.

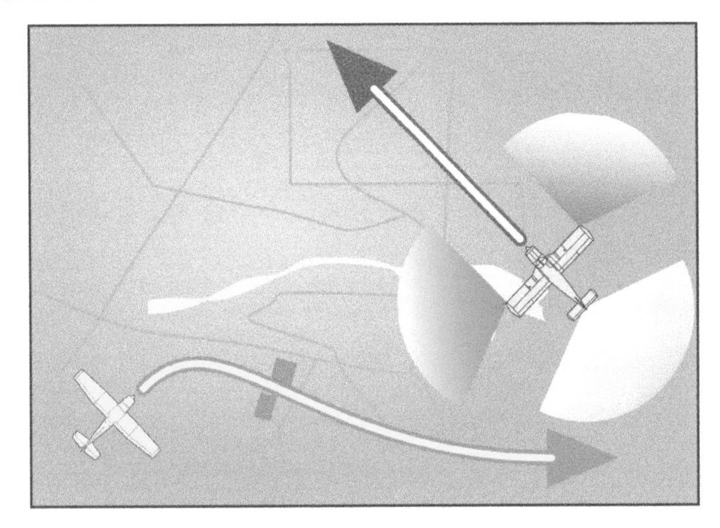

Further Reference: PPL2 Operational Procedures>Operation of Aircraft>Lights to be Displayed by Aircraft *and*
PPL2 Air Law>Rules of the Air>Rules for Avoiding Collisions *and* Rights of Way in Flight

Air Law paper 2 Q16 Answer B

In terms of the definition of an accident, the key points are that the occurrence takes place between the time that any person boards the aircraft with the intention of flight, until all such persons have disembarked. An accident can include a situation where a person is killed or injured either in or on the aircraft, or by direct contact with the aircraft, including parts which have become detached from an aircraft. Therefore, for example, a death on an aircraft that occurs while it is in a hangar with no intention of being flown is not reportable under these regulations, but a broken foot caused by something falling off an aircraft as it is pushed-back for departure would be.

Further Reference: PPL2 Operational Procedures>Accident and Incident Investigation>Definitions

Air Law paper 3 Q1 Answer A

Aerodrome information signs (for example taxiway directions etc) should be coloured yellow and back (either yellow background and black inscription, or black background with yellow inscription).

Mandatory signs (for example "No Entry") are red background with white inscription.

Further Reference: PPL2 Air Law>Rules of the Air>Taxiway Signals and Markings

Air Law paper 3 Q2 Answer B

Article 32 (Licences of Personnel) of the Chicago Convention (Convention on International Civil Aviation) states in part "*The pilot and crew of every aircraft engaged in international navigation must have certificates of competency and licences issued or validated by the state in which the aircraft is registered.*"

Further Reference: PPL2 Air Law>Legislation>Basis of Aviation Law

Air Law paper 3 Q3 Answer C

The emergency transponder codes have been previously listed. The transponder code 7500 is used to indicate 'unlawful interference' - also known as a hijack situation.

Further Reference: PPL2 Communications>En-route Procedures>Use of Transponder

Air Law paper 3 Q4 Answer C

In accordance with ICAO Annex 13, "*The sole objective of* the investigation of an accident or incident *shall be the prevention of accidents and incidents. It is not the purpose of this activity to apportion blame or liability.*"

Further Reference: PPL2 Operational Procedures>Accident and Incident Investigation>Definitions

Air Law paper 3 Q5 Answer B

A VFR flight approaching or departing from an airfield outside controlled airspace will normally use the appropriate 'QNH' altimeter setting (so that the altimeter reads 'altitude') for the purposes of obstacle clearance and remaining clear of controlled airspace where the base of controlled airspace is defined as an altitude.

'Transition altitude' is defined as the altitude at or below which the vertical position of an aircraft is controlled by reference to altitudes (meaning that the altimeter must be set to the appropriate QNH).

All the other answer options for this question are incorrect.

Further Reference: PPL2 Air Law>Rules of the Air and Air Traffic Services>Altimeter Setting Procedures

Air Law paper 3 Q6 Answer B

Actual separation of IFR and VFR flights only takes place in Class B airspace. Within Class D airspace IFR flights are separated from other IFR flights, but are given information about VFR flights - separation is not guaranteed (although ATC do try to keep aircraft apart!).

Further Reference: PPL2 Air Law>Division of Airspace and Air Traffic Services>Airspace Summary

Air Law paper 3 Q7 Answer D

The objectives of Air Traffic Services are defined as being to:

- Prevent collisions between aircraft
- Prevent collisions between aircraft on the manoeuvring area and obstructions on that area
- Expedite and maintain an orderly flow of air traffic
- Provide advice and information of the safe and efficient conduct of flights
- Notify organisations of aircraft in need of search and rescue aid, and assist such organisations

Further Reference: PPL2 Air Law>Division of Airspace and Air Traffic Services>Air Traffic Services

Air Law paper 3 Q8 Answer C

ICAO document 4444 (Rules of the Air and Air Traffic Services) states that if an air traffic control clearance is not suitable to the pilot-in-command of an aircraft, that pilot may request, and if practical obtain, an amended clearance.

Further Reference: PPL2 Air Law>Rules of the Air and Air Traffic Services>Area Control Service

Air Law paper 3 Q9 Answer A

The 'special purpose' transponder codes are summarised below:

Code	Meaning
7700	Emergency condition
7600	Radio failure
7500	Unlawful interference

Further Reference: PPL2 Air Law>Rules of the Air>Distress Difficulty and Urgency Signals

Air Law paper 3 Q10 Answer A

The rules on crediting of flight time state that, unless otherwise specified, flight time to be credited for a licence or rating shall have been flown in the same category of aircraft for which the licence or rating is sought.

Further Reference: PPL2 Air Law>JAA/EASA Regulations>JAA Regulations – General

Air Law paper 3 Q11 Answer D

Two or more white crosses displayed on a runway or taxiway, with each arm at an angle of 45° to the runway or taxiway centre line, signify a section of taxiway or runway unfit for the movement of aircraft.

Further Reference: PPL2 Air Law>Rules of the Air>Runways

Air Law paper 3 Q12 Answer B

The table of light signals to aircraft is reproduced below:

ATC Light Signals to Aircraft on Ground

STOP
STOP
GET OFF GET OFF
Move clear of runway
GO
You may take-off
OK TAXI OK TAXI
OK to Taxi
COME BACK COME BACK
Return to starting point

ATC Light Signals to Aircraft in the Air

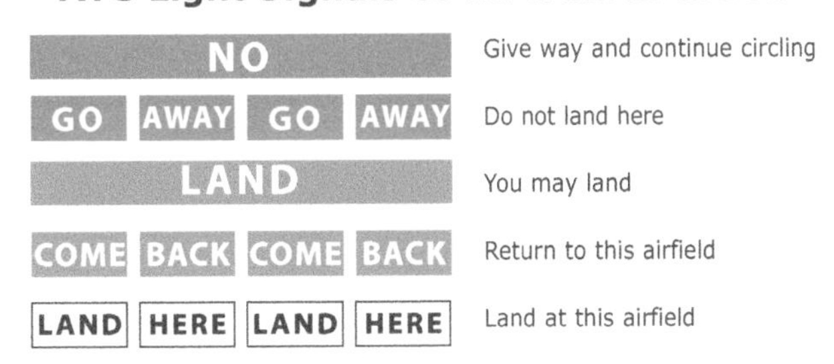

NO
Give way and continue circling
GO AWAY GO AWAY
Do not land here
LAND
You may land
COME BACK COME BACK
Return to this airfield
LAND HERE LAND HERE
Land at this airfield

Further Reference: PPL2 Air Law>Rules of the Air>Light Signals

Air Law paper 3 Q13 Answer C

The holder of a PPL (A) must not fly as pilot in command of such an aeroplane carrying passengers unless within the preceding 90 days he or she has made three take-offs and three landings as the sole manipulator of the controls of an aeroplane of the same type or class.

Note that answer A is not correct because the take-offs and landings must have been made in an aircraft "*...of the same type or class...*".

Further Reference: PPL2 Air Law>JAA/EASA Regulations>Private Pilot Licence (Aeroplane)

Air Law paper 3 Q14 Answer A

The table of search and rescue signals for use by survivors is reproduced below:

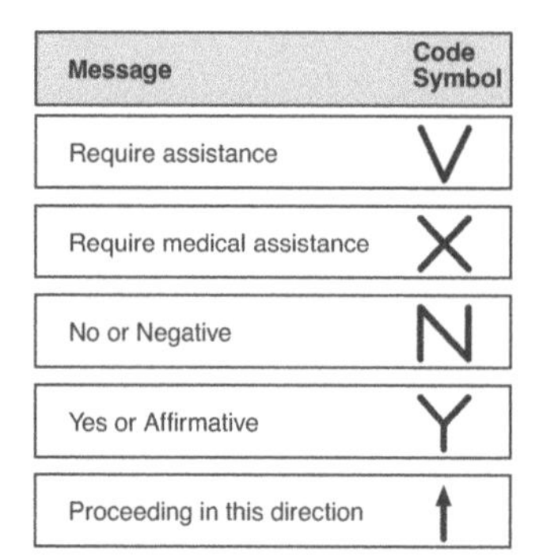

Message	Code Symbol
Require assistance	V
Require medical assistance	X
No or Negative	N
Yes or Affirmative	Y
Proceeding in this direction	↑

Further Reference: PPL2 Operational Procedures>Search and Rescue>Search and Rescue Signals

Air Law paper 3 Q15 Answer A

The 'Mode C' feature of an aircraft's transponder is usually selected using the 'ALT' selection on the transponder. Mode C will transmit the aircraft's pressure altitude – that is the vertical level based on the 1013hPa pressure setting, in other words the aircraft's Flight Level.

It is recommended that where a transponder has the mode C/ALT feature, this should always be selected unless ATC specifically request the aircraft to turn it off.

Further Reference: PPL2 Communications>En-route Procedures>Use of Transponder

Air Law paper 3 Q16 Answer D

An aircraft which has right of way "*... shall maintain its heading and speed.*"

Further Reference: PPL2 Air Law>Rules of the Air>Rules for Avoiding Collisions

	Paper 1				Paper 2				Paper 3			
	A	B	C	D	A	B	C	D	A	B	C	D
1												
2												
3												
4												
5												
6												
7												
8												
9												
10												
11												
12												
13												
14												
15												
16												

Intentionally Left Blank